text by Margriet Ruurs   artwork by Robert Bateman

ROBERT BATEMAN
THE BOY WHO PAINTED NATURE

ORCA BOOK PUBLISHERS

EVEN WHEN he was quite small, Bobby was in awe of nature.

While others played baseball, he scooped
up tadpoles, studied their wiggly shapes and
released them back into the pond so they
could grow into fat frogs.

"Look at the red feathers on that bird's head," he said.

He bought a field guide to help him identify birds.

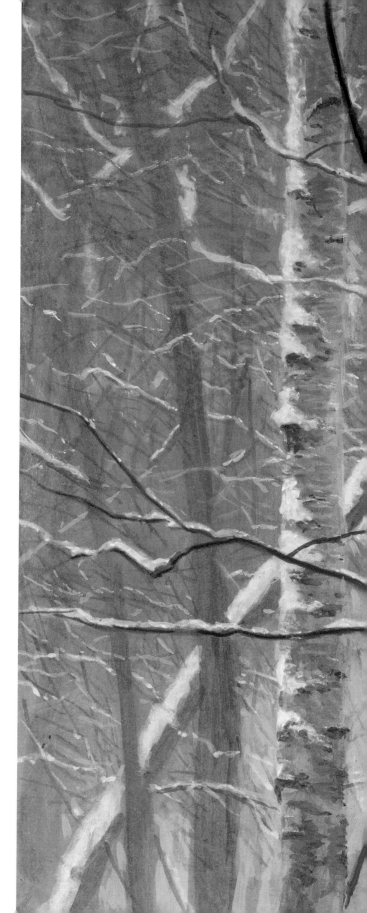

Robert Bateman 2001

He roamed the ravine, noticing the different greens of leaves. His mother bought him a paint box, and he tried to get the colors just right.

Bobby drew birds. He painted deer
and squirrels and even more birds.

In school he spent a lot of time staring out the window.

He dreamed of traveling so he could see more wildlife, from whales to wrens.

As Bobby grew into Bob, he learned the names of plants and animals.

He painted the shapes and patterns of the world around him.

He carved wood into birds, noticing the details of feathers and form. He drew tracks of a deer and followed a rabbit's trail.

© Robert Bateman. 1978.

As soon as he could, Robert traveled the world.
He studied bears...

owls, feathers, moss and wood that had
been polished by waves.

He painted penguins in Antarctica...

and polar bears in the Arctic.

© Robert Bateman-1978.

Robert Bateman
2014

In Africa he observed lions...

and elephants. He painted them as well so that others could see their splendor.

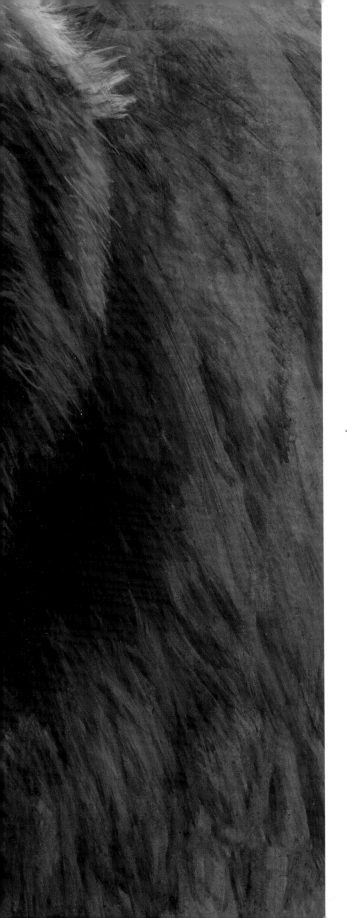

Robert married and had a family. He became a teacher, and all the while he painted.

Soon princes and presidents wanted to own his paintings.

To share the beauty of bears in a rain forest with more people, prints of his paintings were made. These prints showed nature seen through Robert's eyes to everyone, not just those who could buy an original painting.

And his birds seemed to fly off the canvas, right into the hearts of people all over the world. Robert brought animals to life for those who would never get to see them.

Robert Bateman—2009©

Now Robert walks the forest with his grandchildren. He shows them the shape of a leaf, the texture of bark.

He tells them to pay attention to the details of nature all around them.

He picks up a feather, and when his grandchildren notice its softness and curve, he helps them to draw and paint the beauty of nature.

I can't conceive of anything being more varied and rich and handsome than planet Earth. And its crowning beauty is the natural world. I want to soak it up, to understand it as well as I can, and to absorb it. And then I like to put it together and express it in my paintings. This is the way I want to dedicate my work.

—ROBERT BATEMAN

ROBERT IN HIS STUDIO

About Robert Bateman

Robert Bateman strongly believes in spending time outdoors. As a painter of the natural world, he knows the importance of connecting with one's environment.

Born on May 24, 1930, in Toronto, Ontario, Robert now lives in British Columbia. As a boy he spent a lot of time at the Royal Ontario Museum (ROM) in downtown Toronto. He studied the painting techniques used by Andrew Wyeth and the Group of Seven and painted constantly.

Robert has visited every continent. These travels helped him learn about and appreciate the importance of people and nature. His work as an artist and as an advocate for environmental protection has been recognized by the Audubon Society, which named him a "hero of conservation" for the twentieth century. Robert is an Officer of the Order of Canada, and he has received a World Wildlife Fund Member of Honour Award, the Governor General's Award for Conservation and a Royal Canadian Geographical Society Gold Medal.

He has lived in British Columbia since 1985. The newly formed Robert Bateman Foundation supports the Robert Bateman Centre in Victoria, BC. The gallery houses the largest permanent collection of Bateman's art, showcasing the major themes of his life's work, including early experimentation with abstract art styles, his travels throughout the world and his personal commentary on the state of our planet. A place for creative thinking and networking about in-nature education initiatives, the centre also offers inquiry-based education programs for school-aged children, runs a Nature Near You student art contest and hosts a nature sketch club for adults and kids.

From his home on Salt Spring Island, BC, Robert continues to paint and explore the world around him every day and uses his position as one of Canada's most distinguished artists to advocate for nature.

ROBERT AND FAMILY IN EAST AFRICA

Wilson's Storm Petrel
Drake Passage
1978

x2

Rt. Leg
x2

Flat surface

Rt. foot

European Woodcock
Wiltshire
June 1979